# Attention Deficit Disorder

## ADD SYNDROME

DALE R. JORDAN

8700 Shoal Creek Boulevard
Austin, Texas 78758

Printed in the United States of America

**Library of Congress Cataloging-in-Publication Data**

Jordan, Dale R.
   Attention deficit disorder.

   "Published by arrangement with Modern Education
Corporation"—T.p. verso.
   Bibliography: p.
   1. Attention deficit disorders. I. Title.
RJ496.A86J67   1988        618.92'8589        88-15118
ISBN 0-89079-176-7

pro·ed

8700 Shoal Creek Boulevard
Austin, Texas 78758

10   9   8   7   6   5   4   3              89   90   91   92

# CONTENTS

iii

# Author's Preface

*"In a time of drastic change,
it is the learners who inherit the future.
The learned usually find themselves equipped
to live in a world that no longer exists."*

### Eric Hoffer

from BETWEEN THE DEVIL AND THE DRAGON (Harper and Row)

The rather new concept of Attention Deficit Disorder is pressing educators, counselors, and parents hard. It is difficult to comprehend how bright youngsters could still be as immature as children several years below their age. The largely invisible problem we now call ADD Syndrome challenges many of the cherished concepts held for several generations by professionals. We cannot meet this new challenge by clinging to old ideas or attitudes. Seeing Attention Deficit Disorder calls for new eyes. Dealing with it successfully requires new levels of compassion and flexibility. Those who are not open to new knowledge may, as Hoffer implies, sadly find themselves living in a diagnostic and therapeutic world that no longer meets the needs of this very special population. It is my hope that this discussion of Attention Deficit Disorder will stimulate new, creative thinking in how to treat these precious strugglers more successfully.

Dale R. Jordan, Ph.D.
Jordan Diagnostic Center
5700 North Portland
Oklahoma City, OK 73112

# Attention Deficit Disorder

## CHAPTER ONE:

## The Four Forms of ADD Syndrome

In 1985 a rather astonishing fact was reported by the Mental Health Letter published by the Harvard Medical School: almost half of all childhood referrals made to mental health agencies are for Attention Deficit Disorder. Before the 1980s other labels had been used for this frequent problem: Minimal Brain Dysfunction (MBD); hyperactivity; hyperkinesis; "learning disability"; short attention span; immaturity. During the rapid changes in the American culture following World War II, educators began to remark about the inattentive child in the classroom. During the 1950s it seemed that our schools were filling up with youngsters who did not or could not pay attention. Educators began to focus upon students who were too easily distractible, could not tune out the edges and concentrate on the middle of their environment, could not follow a series of instructions without being reminded, could not fit successfully into a group, and so forth. Distractibility and short attention span became prominent topics at meetings where school leaders discussed their frustrations.

The concept of "minimal brain dysfunction" or MBD was born during the 1960s, largely because of the influence of a thoughtful specialist, Dr. Samuel Clements (6). MBD referred to a certain type of child who listened poorly, remembered details poorly, could not follow through without supervision, quickly forgot what was learned, became overly frustrated too easily, could not tolerate normal classroom pressure, and was hyperactive. Skill development in the basic subjects of reading, phonics, spelling, math, and language was spotty and unpredictable. What this child knew on Tuesday was likely forgotten or confused by

1

Wednesday. These children were overly irritable under stress that was normally absorbed by their agemates. MBD youngsters were impulsive and often destructive, having no sense of how to handle things gently. They were compulsive and demanding in a self-centered way, clamoring to satisfy whims of the moment. They were dubbed the "now children," demanding that wishes be satisfied now, not later. They were hyperactive, impulsive, compulsive, irritable, poorly organized, self-centered youngsters who were often medicated by cortical stimulants, such as Ritalin, which frequently reduced their behavior to "normal" levels.

This concept of "minimal brain dysfunction" answered an important question of the 1960s. It helped educators understand that certain underachievers were neurologically different, and that this physical difference was the cause of such irregular behavior. MBD children were regarded as a special population who needed special treatment within the educational arena. They could not be incorporated into traditional classrooms where standard materials and methodology were used. MBD youngsters must be handled differently because they WERE different. This model of "minimal brain dysfunction" played a major part in the development of special education programs during the late 1960s and 1970s. MBD students were placed in self-contained classrooms that were largely isolated from the mainstream educational program. It was often assumed that an MBD child would always be that way to a large degree. The purpose of special education was not to change the child but to help the handicapped student get ready to cope with the world in years to come.

In this isolated environment where learning specialists could interact more intensely with struggling learners, a significant pattern began to be seen. By the late 1970s it was recognized that not all children who displayed the MBD pattern were hyperactive. The earmark of hyperactivity did not apply to all of the underachievers who had poor listening ability, short retention of learned information, and low tolerance for stress. It became apparent that being hyperactive was not a reliable criterion for identifying a child with "minimal brain dysfunction." It also became apparent that at certain age levels, some MBD children began to change. Over a period of time, skill development increased remarkably, along with increased social success. As these children entered puberty, the original cluster of learning disability symptoms began to disappear. Educators realized that a new point of view must be developed to account for the "minimal brain dysfunction" children who were not hyperactive and who began to outgrow most of their learning struggle at a certain point.

For many years the point of reference in clinical diagnosis of mental and emotional problems has been the Diagnostic and Statistical Manual (DSM) of the American Psychiatric Association (APA). During the late 1970s the APA was revising the clinical definitions and categories of mental and emotional illness for a new edition of the Diagnostic and Statistical Manual (1). When DSM III was published in February, 1980, a fundamental change was presented in how clinicians could interpret behavior patterns related to short attention and inability to maintain integrated thought patterns. Instead of the old umbrella concept of "minimal brain dysfunction," the new American Psychiatric Association definitions provided three categories for interpreting the underachiever:

### ATTENTION DEFICIT DISORDER
**314.01 Attention Deficit Disorder with Hyperactivity**
**314.00 Attention Deficit Disorder without Hyperactivity**
**314.80 Attention Deficit Disorder, Residual Type**

Suddenly those involved with educating the underachiever had a new model for interpreting this academic and behavioral problem. Some underachievers were hyperactive; many were not. Most underachievers would gradually outgrow much of the syndrome; some would not. During the developmental years of adolescence, most ADD Syndrome children would progressively overcome much of the symptoms if certain kinds of help were provided. Some would not. Some ADD Syndrome children would become ADD Syndrome adults, not having outgrown the patterns that complicated their early years so much. **But not all of these difficult youngsters are hyperactive.** This change in diagnostic point of view has proved to be a critical factor in recognizing the prevalence of neurologically based learning problems in the classroom.

ADD Syndrome is often complicated by other kinds of learning/behavior problems that are intertwined in the way the student handles new information. Many ADD Syndrome children are also dyslexic (9, 10, 11). Not only are their thought patterns loose and poorly organized, they tend to reverse symbols, scramble any information that goes in a certain sequence, have poor memory for spelling, and stumble over reading. ADD Syndrome students often have poor eye muscle coordination that interferes with accurate focusing of the eyes together as a team (9, 10). Late physical maturity is often seen, which causes social problems and difficulty fitting into groups of peers. Hyperactive ADD Syndrome youngsters are often allergic to certain food substances. These cytotoxic elements in the diet send them into orbit with extreme hyperactive reaction triggered by what they eat or drink (3, 15, 17, 20). Few ADD Syndrome children have just one specific problem. Multiple factors usually must be taken into account to work with these youngsters successfully.

Various professional opinions exist as to what causes ADD Syndrome. There is growing evidence that the pattern is inherited. Most children with this problem also have relatives with similar problems. Biochemical research has revealed that the chemistry of the brain is different in ADD Syndrome. The myelin sheath that surrounds nerve tissues within the normal brain seems to be delayed in reaching full maturity in children with Attention Deficit Disorder. The nerve pathways within the brain are therefore unable to function in a mature way. Thought patterns and mental images are mixed and incomplete because the physical construction of the brain is immature and different. It now appears that ADD Syndrome is caused by physical differences within the brain, and it often runs in families (8, 10, 11, 13).

## ADD Syndrome with Hyperactivity (DSM III 314.01)

The most obvious form of ADD Syndrome is the hyperactive form. No one who deals with a hyperactive, poorly organized child misses the fact that something is wrong. Yet it appears that fewer than half of all ADD children are hyperactive (9, 10, 11). Because most of them are above average in intelligence, mental age is usually far ahead of social maturity and the ability to carry out responsibility. The hyperactive child with loose thought patterns is usually bright. The problem is that such good intelligence is not available for organized use. The following behavior patterns are earmarks of ADD Syndrome with Hyperactivity:

### Short Attention

This child cannot hold full attention on any formal school related task for more than a few seconds at a time. As the child listens to new information or receives a set of instructions, attention begins to break down. The child begins to dart off on rabbit trails. Within a short time the attention has become fixed upon something else, not upon what the child started to do. The hyperactive ADD Syndrome child is like a mosquito, zipping about the environment, flitting rapidly from one point of attention to another. Dr. Ray Wunderlich has described these youngsters as being like bullets that "ricochet" off the environment. (20) It is impossible for them to maintain full attention long enough to do what adults expect. Thought patterns are too loose and too poorly organized to let them concentrate on the same issue long enough to finish the task.

## Easily Distracted

It is impossible for the hyperactive ADD Syndrome child to ignore what goes on nearby. The attention zips to nearby movement to see what is going on. The child's attention darts toward any sound to find out what is happening. An unusual odor is an irresistable attraction, and the child must see where the smell is coming from. A change in temperature or an unexpected puff of air captures the attention, jerking it away from the main responsibility. Pressure of clothing demands immediate satisfaction with a lot of scratching and tugging at garments to relieve the sensation. Moments of skin itch become the main point of concern, and the itch must be scratched. Feelings within the body as gas bubbles work through the abdominal area or a belch erupts cannot be ignored. Any change, anything new or different in the child's environment, calls for immediate investigation. Hyperactive ADD Syndrome children cannot ignore these intrusions into their sensory awareness.

## Poor Listening

Hyperactive ADD Syndrome youngsters cannot stay on track in listening. When a flow of oral information comes their way, they cannot absorb the full message. Only bits and pieces of what they hear remain firmly fixed in the memory. When the listening experience is over, the child clamors: "What? What did you say?" There is no retention of what was just explained or described. Most hyperactive ADD Syndrome students fully understand only part of what they hear at school or at home. As a rule, less than 30% of the full oral message is absorbed and retained (9, 10). Later they exclaim: "You didn't tell me that!" or "I didn't hear you say that!" Listening to a stream of oral information is exceedingly poor for these youngsters.

## Unfinished Business

Hyperactive ADD Syndrome children do not finish what they start. No task is completed unless a great deal of supervision and reminding is done by adults. On his or her own, the child starts many projects but finishes none. Only part of a work page is completed, yet the child is certain that all of it was done. Only some of the math problems have been worked, but the child believes that the whole page was finished. Only part of the material was copied from the board, but the child is convinced that all of it was copied. ADD Syndrome children are forever losing things. Homework assignments that were completed under the parents' supervision are lost before they reach school the next day. Books, pencils, and workbooks disappear from the child's work space or locker. Jackets, caps, and play equipment vanish. Teeth are only partly brushed. Hair is only partly shampooed. Baths are left unfinished. Chores are started, but not completed. The hyperactive ADD Syndrome child is too scattered to go completely from start to finish unless firm supervision is imposed.

## Impulsivity

The hyperactive ADD Syndrome child does not think ahead. There is no postponing a wish or desire. The child demands it *now*. He or she wants it *now*. No thought is given to consequences. No pondering is done as to what the effect will be if the impulse is satisfied at this moment. The impulsive child has tunnel vision, seeing only what he or she wants now. Everything else is shut out of consideration. The child does not recognize how satisfying the impulse now will affect or inconvenience others. No notice is given to possible destruction that might occur in satisfying the desire of the moment. Hyperactive ADD Syndrome children who bump and knock things around simply do not realize what they are doing to their environment. They do not connect the consequences with the action.

## Poor Organization

It is impossible for the hyperactive ADD Syndrome child to organize. The ingredients of the situation do not come together into an organized whole. This child does not see a cluttered room with things tossed every which way. He or she locks in on only a few of the items and does not see the rest. The child is bewildered when adults demand that "this mess must be cleaned up." The hyperactive ADD Syndrome child does not see a mess. Teachers demand that the desk be kept in a more orderly way, but the child does not see a state of disorder. The parts do not connect within the child's mental image to form a whole. The child deals with parts, not wholes. The concept of organization does not exist for most hyperactive ADD Syndrome youngsters unless it is imposed by someone from the outside.

## Disruptiveness

Because the hyperactive ADD Syndrome child does not plug into his or her whole environment, there is no awareness of the usual social amenities. When a thought comes to mind, the child blurts it out. When an itch occurs, the child scratches noisily. When things need to be moved, the child does so loudly with exaggerated motions and commotion. When turns must be taken, the child bursts ahead of others. When things must be shared, the child grabs instead of waiting. The hyperactive ADD Syndrome child is noisy, intrusive, and insensitive to the rights of others. He or she does not see the space markers that help any group maintain good order. The child barges in without noticing that he or she should stay out. The child reaches into another person's territory without paying attention to the signals that he or she is not welcome. The hyperactive ADD Syndrome child does not see the usual courteous ways of fitting into a group. Any group activity is disrupted by impulsive, spontaneous behavior that is seldom self-contained. This child puts a great deal of pressure upon those who must share his or her space.

## Body Energy Overflow

The body of a hyperactive ADD Syndrome child is never completely at rest. Motor signals that tell muscles to work continually overflow. Feet scrub the floor. Legs drum the sides of the desk. Hands roam the area finding things to handle. Bodies thrash about in chairs. Loud sighs and vocal noises emerge inadvertently. Pencils clack against the desk top. Books topple with a thud to the floor. Paper is ripped from a tablet with too much force. The whole body may begin to rock in an overflow rhythm that causes the chair to squeak or grind. The body of a hyperactive ADD Syndrome student cannot be still longer than brief periods of time. It is impossible for the child to stop the energy overflow. If gum chewing is permitted, the child smacks and slurps. If snacks are served, food is spilled on the table and floor. If quiet time is supposed to be observed, the child is up and out of the chair several times. The body is in some kind of motion most of the time, even during sleep. The next morning the bed looks like it hosted a wrestling match during the night. This kinetic overflow is inadvertent, usually beyond the conscious will of the child.

## Emotional Overflow

The hyperactive ADD Syndrome child does not fit successfully into groups. He or she almost never is a successful member of a class. The child is much less mature than most of the peers. Academic skills are usually behind schedule, leaving the child unable to compete or earn praise. More mature classmates complain that he or she "acts like a baby."

Outbursts of anger are common and, over a period of time, explosions involving tears occur frequently. When the child is compared with classmates who are learning new skills on schedule, he or she is seen as immature, irritable, disruptive, demanding, and uncooperative. The group soon becomes tired of this pattern and rejects the child, who ends up outside the group as an outcast. Being a misfit is one of the usual plights of the hyperactive ADD Syndrome student whose emotions flood the scene with little self-control.

## Insatiability

An earmark of many hyperactive ADD Syndrome children is insatiability. Cravings are never fully satisfied. Enough is never obtained. Attention from the teacher or parent is never as much as the child needs or wants. Playmates become exhausted from constant demands for more. There is an irrational component in these insatiable demands. The child does not respond to common sense reasoning. He or she does not understand when the adult says: "You have had enough." The demand is for more. The clamor is: "Let's do it again." The c·y is: "He got a bigger piece than I got." The child is a pain to take shopping because he or she clamors for everything in the store. This child tends to be jealous, accusing others of not giving him or her a fair share. In the family, this child accuses parents of loving others more. The emotional needs of the hyperactive ADD Syndrome child can be a bottomless pit that cannot be filled. No matter how much love and affection are bestowed, it is not enough. The child whines and badgers and pleads for more.

## Blame of Others

Because the hyperactive ADD Syndrome child does not perceive the whole but deals only with disorganized parts, he or she does not see the normal chain of cause and effect. There is no organized perception of what caused an event to take place. It is always the fault of someone else. The cat broke the vase, or the neighbor broke the window. Sister Ann made the mess in the kitchen, or brother John left the towels on the bathroom floor. Mom made the child late to school. The teacher did not explain the assignment to the class. The bell rang too early for books to be found in the locker. The prices were too high at the store, so that is why all of the allowance was gone the second day. Blame of others is often a complicating factor when dealing with the hyperactive ADD Syndrome youngster.

## Overreaction to Criticism

It is almost impossible for the hyperactive ADD Syndrome youngster to handle constructive criticism. The child does not see the purpose of the criticism. He or she locks in on only the sound of the words, the tone of the adult's voice, or red marks on the paper. This over-sensitivity often leads to a paranoid attitude in later years. The hyperactive ADD Syndrome child has unrealistic expectations, confidently expecting that the next task will be done well. When it is left unfinished, or when important items are omitted, the child bursts into self-defense rather than hearing what the critic has to say. It is difficult for leaders to handle this over-sensitivity successfully.

## ADD Syndrome without Hyperactivity (DSM III 314.00)

At least half of all ADD Syndrome children appear *not* to be hyperactive (8, 9, 10). In fact, many of these struggling learners tend to be quiet and passive, not attracting attention to themselves the way hyperactive youngsters advertise their struggle. The following behavior patterns are earmarks of ADD Syndrome without Hyperactivity.

## Drifting Away from the Task

The hyperactive child darts off on rabbit trails, kicking up disruptive dust that attracts everyone's attention. The passive ADD Syndrome child drifts away quietly. A casual observer sees no telltale signs that the mind has wandered. A close observer sees a far away look in the eyes as if the child is off in another world. But the body is usually still. This quiet drifter can float for long periods of time, not learning new material or absorbing new knowledge, before adults are aware of the problem. These children are often called "star gazers," or "day dreamers." No matter how hard they try to stay on task, their attention drifts away. Thought patterns are too loose to let them hold onto their first mental images over a period of time.

## Loose Thought Patterns

It is impossible for ADD Syndrome children to maintain tight, well organized thought patterns. Information in sequence becomes cluttered and scrambled. Important pieces of information drop out, leaving gaps in the mental image. Steps that should be followed in a certain order become scrambled and mixed together. Information that has been learned does not appear on the "mental screen" when it is needed. New information does not become connected or integrated with what has already been learned. Memory patterns are too loose to let the student do groups of things well. For example, several spelling words may be written correctly, then suddenly the child misses the next several words in the list. The first few math problems may be worked correctly, then he or she starts to make mistakes in the next several problems. There is a "short circuit" quality in the way the child thinks, remembers, and analyzes.

## Shift of First Impressions

ADD Syndrome children do not hold onto first impressions. In sounding out words, the first impression may be correct, then it changes within the child's mind, causing the first impression to seem wrong. The child spends a great deal of work time erasing and changing what was written first. Math problems that were correct suddenly seem incorrect. Impressions of what is seen and heard do not stay together. Soon the child is confused by the jumbled impressions that at first seemed clear and accurate.

## Time Lag

The central nervous system of ADD Syndrome children often does not deliver needed information on schedule. It is not unusual for many seconds or several minutes to go by before a full mental image is developed. These children spend long periods of time pondering, searching the memory, and trying it several different ways. It is impossible for them to speed up the rate at which the central nervous system processes information. They have no choice but to sit and wait. As they wait, they tend to drift, which greatly complicates performance problems. These students often whisper over and over to themselves, quietly rehearsing until all of the pieces fit together. They need to count fingers in math or touch their work as they figure things out. School work is time consuming and exhausting for them.

## Trouble Naming and Describing

Loose memory patterns make it impossible for the ADD Syndrome child to recall precise terminology the moment it is needed. For example, names of geometric shapes continually mix together or disappear completely, leaving the child with a shape that he misnames or cannot name. Names of math signs disappear, leaving the child groping for what to say. Terminology in science and social studies evaporates, leaving the child stuck with only half an answer. What to say, what to call things, how to describe an event — these tasks are frustrating and difficult for the ADD Syndrome child. Standardized test scores, especially intelligence tests that are time limited, are often much lower than the actual knowledge level. When the child has all the time he or she needs to search and ponder, adults are often surprised at the sophisticated knowledge the ADD Syndrome struggler

13

actually has. On-the-spot demand for an answer often leaves this child unable to respond.

## Oral Footnoting

ADD Syndrome listeners often make oral footnotes as they follow a stream of oral information. In order to anchor specific details of what they hear, they respond with vocal sounds, short words, or partial repeating of what they are hearing. In listening to a set of instructions, and ADD Syndrome listener might say: "OK ... um ... yeah ... OK ... yes ... um ... OK." This goes on while the speaker talks. Or the oral message might be paraphrased: "Turn the knob ... on twelve ... close it ... five times." This provides a quick repeat digest of what has just been heard. Sometimes the ADD Syndrome listener turns statements into questions:

| | |
|---|---|
| Speaker: | Open your book to page ninety-seven... |
| ADD Listener: | Ninety-seven? |
| Speaker: | Now, start with the first paragraph. |
| ADD Listener: | First paragraph? |
| Speaker: | Now copy the first line. |
| ADD Listener: | Copy it? |

For many ADD Syndrome students, this oral feedback (making oral footnotes) is an essential part of understanding what they hear. It is impossible for these students to develop full mental images of oral information without making a vocal response. This is actually a form of multi-sensory compensation. By hearing it and saying it, they combine two sensory pathways simultaneously. This is often enough to create a firm mental image which they can hold long enough

14

to use what they have just heard. If oral footnoting is forbidden, these students are helpless to interpret and retain what they have received through listening.

### ADD Syndrome, Residual Type (DSM III 314.80)

Approximately 80% of all ADD Syndrome children begin to outgrow their symptoms during puberty (9, 10). Onset of puberty usually brings brain chemistry into better balance. Hormone production during puberty usually increases the maturity of the myelin structure, which is essential for good thought processing within the brain. It is important to visualize ADD Syndrome along an index line that shows level of severity:

| 0 | 1 2 3 | 4 5 6 7 | 8 9 10 |
|---|-------|---------|--------|
| none | mild | moderate | severe |

For approximately 80% of all ADD Syndrome children, the level of severity declines as puberty advances. For example, a hyperactive ADD Syndrome child at Age 7½ might be at Level 9 (middle of the severe range). As physical maturity begins around Age 12, he or she might be down to Level 8 (low side of the severe range). By Age 14, after two years of hormone activity within the central nervous system, severity might be down to Level 7 (high side of the moderate range). By Age 18 the student might be down to Level 6 (middle of the moderate range). By early 20s he or she might be down to Level 5 or lower. For most ADD Syndrome students, physical maturation steadily improves the ability of the central nervous system to handle school learning.

Unfortunately, approximately 20% of all ADD Syndrome individuals do not outgrow their symptoms (10). **ADD Syn-**

15

**drome, Residual Type**, manifests the following characteristics:

## Poor Organization

The ADD Syndrome adult may or may not still be hyperactive. A majority of the hyperactive children outgrow most of that pattern, regardless of whether they outgrow other ADD Syndrome characteristics. One of the most striking earmarks of residual ADD Syndrome is poor organization in adults. These men and women are poorly organized in most ways. They are habitually late to appointments and meetings. Job tools or materials tend to be scattered all over the place. Important things are continually lost or misplaced. These adults usually leave a trail of things behind with constant cluttering of work space. Schedules are not followed. Deadlines are not met. Bills are not paid on time. Plans are not followed through. Housekeeping is haphazard. The person's car tends to be filled with "trash" that is seldom emptied. This adult's space is like that of the ADD Syndrome child because the brain does not maintain an organized impression of time, space, or things within a given space.

## Poor Listening

The ADD Syndrome adult is a poor listener. Important oral information is continually misperceived or misunderstood. Oral messages are remembered in a cluttered scrambled way, leaving different impressions than were intended by the speaker. The ADD Syndrome adult does not develop a cumulative mental image as new oral information is received through listening. This person cannot repeat what was just heard without leaving out important chunks or scrambling the order of the information. He or she usually takes poor notes of lectures or discussions. Effort to preserve oral information through notes tends to be incomplete and inadequate. The ADD Syndrome adult is at a distinct disadvantage in listening situations. Telephone messages are misunderstood. Conversations are remembered incorrectly, and radio or television news is misinterpreted. Lectures and sermons are only partly comprehended. Oral instructions are inadvertently changed so that the ADD Syndrome listener starts off doing the task differently than he or she was told. Names of people are misunderstood, and new names of places or things are lost. This adult struggles in any task that requires good listening.

## Emotional Sensitivity

The ADD Syndrome adult tends to be overly sensitive. It is not unusual to find a truly paranoid frame of mind in which the first impulse is to jump to the defensive level instead of hearing what is actually being said. This person has suffered criticism all of his or her life. Childhood ADD Syndrome patterns kept this individual in continual conflict with adult expectations. As the sensitive years of teen-age development occurred, the criticism continued. The ADD Syndrome adult has never known praise that was not mixed with criticism. This person does not have the "emotional toughness" most adults develop during the process of growing up. Constructive criticism tends to trigger emotional outbursts, angry self-defense, and blaming others. The ADD Syndrome adult is often too touchy to have satisfactory relationships with others.

## Short Attention

Becoming adult does not lengthen the attention span of ADD Syndrome, Residual Type. Attention to a given task is short with the tendency to dart away or drift off on rabbit trails. The ADD Syndrome adult has great difficulty with conversation. This person may ask an intelligent question, then dart to another topic before the speaker has uttered half a dozen words. It is highly disconcerting and irritating to try to converse with an ADD Syndrome adult. His or her thought patterns are loose and poorly organized. The attention does not stay fixed longer than a few seconds at a time. This adult is restless in audience situations. No matter whether it is a concert, lecture, a sermon, or a demonstration, the attention darts or drifts away. He or she begins rustling the program or digging noisily into a purse or popcorn bag. There is a lot of sighing, coughing, and throat clearing, which irritates those sitting nearby. He or she shifts around in the seat, causing squeaks and visually blocking whoever is sitting behind. Every few minutes the ADD Syndrome adult bursts into speech, whispering irrelevant things to a neighbor or asking a totally irrelevant question that distracts those nearby. It is virtually impossible for an ADD Syndrome adult to develop deeper appreciation of theater, symphony, opera, or other kinds of activities that require long concentration. This person is blocked from these kinds of satisfying interests because the thought patterns are too loose and short lived.

## Difficulty Telling and Describing

The ADD Syndrome adult often has difficulty organizing his or her mental material in order to tell about an event or describe what happened. Speech is a series of bits and pieces that do not always emerge in the right sequence. Names are lost, the next word comes too slowly, and specific terminology is cluttered. If an ADD Syndrome adult tries to talk rapidly, the result sounds much like a speech defect with poor articulation. Sentences are chopped and scrambled with the point of the story darting here and there. The oral flow reflects the loose, disorganized mental image which the ADD Syndrome adult is trying to verbalize. Essential ingredients tend to be left out of the message. Later this adult is frustrated, even angry, if the listener disagrees or seems not to understand. Emotional over-sensitivity is often triggered when the ADD Syndrome adult thinks that the full message was delivered, but the listener realizes that something essential was scrambled or left out.

## Short Job Tenure

Not all adults who have short job tenure are ADD Syndrome, but many are. It is often impossible for these adults to fit into typical job situations. Incomplete listening comprehension, trouble expressing ideas orally, overly sensitive emotional reaction to criticism, inability to follow a schedule, poor punctuality, and so forth cause many ADD Syndrome adults to be poor job performers. The tendency is for the person to move from job to job frequently, seldom staying with any position longer than a few months.

## Social Misfit

ADD Syndrome adults are seldom able to fit successfully into typical social situations. The cluster of problems involving poor listening, misunderstanding, emotional sensitivity, poor oral expression, short attention, and poor organization keep these persons from plugging into the flow of conversation. A majority of ADD Syndrome adults have very immature social skills. They tend to be isolated within the adult world, not able to blend into the interchange that is necessary for social success. Marriage relationships are difficult unless the spouse is a patient, easy going person who gives plenty of time and is not bothered by poor organization.

## Shoestring Baby Syndrome

Three categories of the APA Diagnostic and Statistical Manual III do not include still another form of Attention Deficit Disorder (9, 10). A certain subgroup within this overall classification can be identified by the following growth patterns.

19

## Low Birth Weight

This does not refer to premature infants, although such children often manifest ADD Syndrome struggle. The Shoestring Baby is a full term infant, arriving within two or three weeks of scheduled delivery. Birth weight is low compared with birth length. Significance is seen when birth length is 19 inches or longer, but birth weight is below seven pounds. Examples of significant ratios that signal high risks for Attention Deficit Disorder are:

| | |
|---|---|
| 19 inches | 5 pounds, 10 ounces |
| 20 inches | 6 pounds, 2 ounces |
| 21 inches | 6 pounds, 6 ounces |

The probability of the child having ADD Syndrome increases as the ratio between birth length and birth weight increases. The longer and "skinnier" the baby, the more likely it is that the child will display prominent ADD Syndrome characteristics later on.

## Problems of Infancy

Shoestring Babies tend to have underdeveloped body systems. For example, they tend to have colic because of lactose intolerance. The digestive system is not mature enough in early infancy to digest milk. After a few months, digestion smooths out as enzyme production becomes stable and colic disappears. Immunity systems are also immature. Shoestring Babies have repeated colds, sore throats, ear infections, bronchial congestion, and often pneumonia. As with the digestive system, these respiratory-type problems diminish as the baby matures. First teeth emerge on schedule in these children, but baby teeth usually do not come out on schedule.

## Problems of Childhood

Shoestring Babies are usually late losing baby teeth. These ADD Syndrome youngsters usually do not lose the first baby teeth until the seventh or eighth year. Children with normal physical maturity should lose lower front baby teeth by age 6½ and upper front baby teeth by age 7. Shoestring Babies tend to be as much as two years behind that developmental schedule. Top front permanent teeth usually signal that all of the body systems are ready to handle classroom learning requirements. Shoestring Babies are as much as two years late reaching this important developmental milestone. There is a high correlation between the age at which the top front permanent teeth emerge and the ability of the child to settle into good classroom listening, do assignments without help, and remember from day to day what is learned. Shoestring Babies (low birth weight ADD Syndrome children) are usually behind this developmental schedule.

## Social Isolation

Shoestring Babies also tend to be late in other important developmental ways. The milestone of puberty is usually behind schedule. A majority of Shoestring Babies do not begin puberty until Age 13½ to 15. This late development is especially difficult for boys. It is often devastating for a late maturing boy in eighth or ninth grade to have to take showers with peers who are fully developed physically. This delayed entry into puberty is often a cultural and emotional shock from which sensitive late bloomers never fully recover. When puberty is delayed, as it is for a majority of these low birthweight youngsters, the social skills of teen years are also delayed. It is not unusual for these late blooming boys to reach their early twenties before voice has fully changed, facial hair is abundant, and full body growth has been completed. These late developers cannot participate in typical teen-age social life, which sharply compounds the problems caused by ADD Syndrome itself.

These are the faces of ADD Syndrome which an alert clinician sees. Those who manifest these patterns are highly frustrated in today's American culture. Self-confidence is usually low because of chronic failure or continual near failure. Self-image is usually low and negative because there has been too little praise and success upon which to build a positive feeling of self. ADD Syndrome students usually have little hope. As they look ahead, the future does not hold much more promise than the past, unless the attention deficit patterns are recognized early enough for help to be extended. ADD Syndrome persons tend to be second class citizens in our competitive society where great emphasis is placed upon rapid achievement. It is critically important that this syndrome be recognized early enough to change the course of failure into success.

## Checklist of ADD Syndrome Patterns

### HYPERACTIVITY
Excessive body activity.
Cannot ignore what goes on nearby.
Cannot say "no" to impulses.
Cannot leave others alone.
Cannot spend time alone without feeling nervous or left out.
Cannot leave things alone.
Cannot keep still or stay quiet.

### PASSIVE BEHAVIOR
Below normal level of body activity.
Reluctant to become involved with group activity.
Tries not to be involved in group discussion.
Avoids answering questions or giving oral responses.
Does not volunteer information.
Prefers to stay alone in play situations.
Avoids being included in games.
Spends long periods of time off in own private world.
Uses fewest words possible when required to talk.

## SHORT ATTENTION

Cannot keep thoughts concentrated longer than a short
period of time.

Continually off on rabbit trails.

Must continually be called back to the task.

Drifts or darts away from task before finishing.

## LOOSE THOUGHT PATTERNS

Cannot maintain organized mental images.

Continually loses important details.

Cannot do a series of things without starting to make
mistakes.

Cannot remember a series of events, facts, or details.

Must have continual help to tell what has happened.

Cannot remember a series of instructions.

Cannot remember assignments over a period of time.

Cannot remember rules of games.

Keeps forgetting names of people and things.

## POOR ORGANIZATION

Cannot keep life organized without help.

Continually loses things

Cannot stay on schedule without supervision.

Cannot remember simple routines from day to day.

Lives in a cluttered space.

Cannot straighten up room or desk without help.

Cannot do homework without supervision.

## CHANGE OF FIRST IMPRESSIONS

First impressions do not stay the same.

Mental images immediately change.

Continual erasing and changing as writing is done.

Has impression that others are "playing tricks" because
things seem to shift and change.

Continually surprised or startled as things seem different.

Word patterns, spelling patterns, math problems seem to
change.

## POOR LISTENING COMPREHENSION

Cannot get the full meaning of what others say.

Continually says "What?" or "What do you mean?" as speaker finishes oral message.

Interrupts speaker by clamoring "What?" or "Huh?" or "What do you mean?"

Cannot follow oral instructions without hearing again.

Needs to have oral information repeated and explained again.

Does not keep on listening.

Drifts or darts away before speaker has finished talking.

Later insists "You didn't say that" or "I didn't hear you say that."

Cannot remember later what speaker said.


## TIME LAG

Long pauses before student reacts.

Does not start assignment without being pushed or guided to start.

Long periods of time go by with no work done. Long pauses while student searches memory.

Much whispering to self as student searches memory for information.

Continually falls behind the pace of group activity.

Does not stay on schedule set by teacher or group.


## OVERLY SENSITIVE

Immediate defensive reaction to criticism or correction. Blames others.

Spends a great deal of emotional energy defending self or blaming others.

Flies into tantrum when criticized.

Jumps the gun, does not wait to receive all of the information before becoming angry or defensive.

Leaders must spend a lot of time restoring calm and soothing hurt feelings.

## UNFINISHED TASKS

Does not finish any task without supervision.

Leaves several unfinished tasks scattered around.

Thinks task is finished when it is not.

Does not realize when more is yet to be done to finish task.


## TROUBLE FITTING IN SOCIALLY

Cannot fit into group situations without conflict.

Whines or clamors for own way.

Fusses about rules not being fair.

Storms out of game when not winning.

Wants to quit and do something else before others are finished.

Is aggressive and domineering in order to get own way.

Cannot carry on small talk as part of social events.

Wanders about, avoiding personal involvement in social gatherings.

Is insensitive to normal manners and protocol.

Tends to be abrupt, rude, impolite in expressing opinions.

Is overly critical of how social events are managed.

Keeps conflict going over unimportant issues.

Displays self-centered attitude instead of noticing needs of others.


## EASILY DISTRACTED

Attention continually darts to whatever is going on nearby.

Cannot ignore nearby events.

Continually stops work to see what others are doing.

Overly aware of nearby sound, odor, movement.

Cannot ignore own body sensations.

Must scratch every itch, adjust clothing, touch or feel objects.


## IMMATURITY

Behavior obviously less mature than expected for that age.

Behaves like much younger person.

Cannot get along well with age mates.

Prefers to play or be with younger persons.

Has interests and thought patterns of much younger persons.

Does not make effort to "grow up."

Refuses to accept responsibility or be responsible.

Behavior is impulsive/compulsive.

Acts on spur of the moment instead of thinking things through.

Refuses long-range goals.

Insists on immediate satisfaction of wishes and desires.

Puts self ahead of others.

Blames others for own mistakes.

Triggers displeasure of companions.

Is often disliked by others.

## INSATIABILITY

Desires are never satisfied.

Clamors for more.

Cannot leave others alone.

Demands attention.

Quickly bored and wants something different.

Complains that others get larger share.

Blames parents and leaders for not being fair.

Drains emotions of those who must be involved with this person's life.

Triggers desire in others to push this person away.

Often dreaded by others.

Becomes target of rejection by others.

## IMPULSIVITY

Does not plan ahead.

Acts on spur of moment.

Does whatever comes to mind.

Shows no common sense in making decisions.

Does not think of consequences.

Demands immediate satisfaction of wishes and desires.

Is a "now" person.
Cannot put off desires or wishes.

## DISRUPTIVENESS

Is disruptive influence in group.
Keeps things stirred up.
Triggers conflict within group.
Disturbs neighbors during study time.
Causes others to complain about how this person is behaving.
Others are relieved when this person is absent.

## BODY ENERGY OVERFLOW

Some part of the body in continual motion.
Cannot sit still.
Cannot be quiet.
Can hold body motions under control briefly, but overflow starts again soon.
Fingers fiddle with things.
Feet scrub floor.
Legs bump desk.
Body shifts around.
Mouth makes noises.

## EMOTIONAL OVERFLOW

Emotions always near the surface.
Cries too easily.
Laughs too loudly.
Squeals too much.
Giggles too often.
Protests too frequently.
Clamors in an emotional way.
Easily triggered into hysterical state.
Tantrums always near the surface.

## LACK OF CONTINUITY

Life does not have continuity.
This person's life is lived in unconnected segments.

This event does not flow into next.

Must have supervision and guidance to stay with a course of action.

Present activity not connected in this person's mind with what happened previously or what will follow.

Daily patterns and routines do not register.

This person continually surprised by each task requirement, no matter how many times routine has been done.

## POOR TELLING AND DESCRIBING

Stumbles over words, names, and specific details while telling.

Speech jumps around without following an organized theme.

Speech made up of fragments instead of whole statements.

## CHAPTER TWO

## ADD Syndrome in the Classroom

Regardless of which type of ADD Syndrome a child might manifest, the basic problem in the classroom is inability to plug into the environment. Whether hyperactive or passive, this child does not absorb the environment in an effective way. New information presented in formal lessons does not enter the memory systems. New experiences within the group do not register as fully meaningful events. Important interactions that give meaning to relationships do not connect. The ADD Syndrome child seldom comprehends more than 30% of what occurs around him or her (9, 10). New vocabulary is not added to the language stock on schedule. New data is not fully recorded by the mind. There is no steady, ongoing growth of skills in academic work or social development. In most ways, this child is a misfit in mainstream classrooms. The underlying inability to devote full attention to what occurs outside the child's self blocks new learning. The ADD Syndrome child cannot fit into the regular world of education. These children bring a cluster of problems into the classroom, creating challenges which teachers cannot always meet.

### Self-Centeredness

Most ADD Syndrome youngsters are likeable in one-to-one relationships. When they are alone with an adult or a playmate, a good relationship often occurs. These children are often deeply sensitive, feeling the same emotions felt by other intelligent youngsters. They care deeply for pets. They grieve over sorrow that comes into the lives of family and friends. They laugh and make jokes and have lots of fun when they are free to set their own pace in working out mental images. One-to-one, an ADD Syndrome child can be as delightful as any other person. But when he or she must enter a group and interact with several others for an extended period of time, a critical breakdown occurs. The ADD Syndrome child spends most of the time dealing with self.

Inattention makes it impossible for the ADD Syndrome child to recognize the need to put self aside in the interest of others. However, these children are not necessarily selfish. Many are generous to a fault in letting others have their things. The problem is that the personality structure is centered around self. This child is preoccupied by personal wishes, usually in the form of make-believe. ADD Syndrome children spend many hours off on private rabbit trails, acting out stories they invent or being heroes in battles they imagine. Quiet ones spend long periods of time adrift in imaginary situations that would make quite remarkable movies. The body is often still with no outward sign of activity, while the mind is busy developing a complicated fantasy scene. Hyperactive ADD Syndrome children act out their inner stories, rocking their chairs, turning furniture upside down for fortresses, "marching" or "dancing" with feet drumming the floor. They begin to hum and mumble dialogues. They thrust swords or punch out an assailant in imaginary Kung Fu battles. This overflow of imagination immediately disrupts the class, calling for disciplinary action from the teacher. But the attention of the child is turned inward where he or she is the star of this private world. Those who eventually outgrow ADD Syndrome gradually stop this sort of self-centered fantasizing, but it is one of the more critical problems faced by teachers in the first several years of formal education. When the child is centered on self, there is little way that student can be an effective member of a classroom group.

During this self-centered phase, the ADD Syndrome child spends most of the time on self-gratification. When do we go to lunch? How much more do we have to do? When can I go home? Did you see my new dress? I got a new ball from my uncle. I can't find my new pencil. I need to go to the restroom. I don't want to do any more work now. When can we go play? You know what I saw last night? These are the concerns of less mature ADD Syndrome youngsters. These kinds of self-centered thoughts occupy most of their time. Formal learning in the classroom cannot penetrate this thicket of self-interest. It requires extraordinary effort on the teacher's part to break through this kind of self-preoccupation in order to implant new academic knowledge and skills. The self-centered ADD Syndrome child is virtually beyond the reach of others except in a one-to-one relationship where tight structure can be maintained by the adult.

## Boredom

When the ADD Syndrome child is pressed into group learning, a strong sense of isolation occurs. The central nervous system is not capable of plugging in the variety of events happening at the same time. Loose thought patterns cannot develop an organized sense of what the whole group is doing. Too many loose ends keep the child from following conversations or discussions well enough to be a responsive member. The ADD Syndrome child cannot deal with a group environment effectively. In reality, the child is isolated from the streams of interaction taking place. Whether hyperactive or passive, this child is alone in the world of formal learning. Oral information given by the teacher to the group does not make sense. The purpose of workbook activities does not register. The child does not enter into the spirit of the group as skills are practiced. The ADD Syndrome child cannot compete successfully, so he or she quickly becomes an outsider in any competitive task. Alone on this island in the stream of learning, the child has nothing meaningful to do. Copying from the board or working a page of math problems is risky and pointless to this child. Caught in a group process that gives little pleasure or few rewards, the child rapidly becomes bored. Fingers go exploring for something to do. Attention wanders to something more interesting. Memory drifts to an experience that was lots of fun. Desire lingers over a wish that has not been fulfilled. Make-believe carries the mind away from the dull classroom into an exciting, rewarding fantasy adventure. Being bored is one of the most commonly felt emotions of the ADD Syndrome child in the classroom.

## Restlessness

Bored bodies soon become restless. With nothing meaningful to do, the ADD Syndrome child soon begins to seek something to do. One of the first signals of lost attention is restlessness, especially with hyperactive youngsters who have short attention. Restlessness creates distraction that intrudes on others. Wiggles cause the chair to shift or squeak. Shifting around in the seat causes noise and movement. Rustling papers or knocking books to the floor attracts attention. Aimlessly rolling the pencil back and forth on the table top or flipping edges of books with a fingernail sends distracting sounds to neighbors. Sighing, groaning, and explosive breathing add to the disruptive body action. Soon nearby classmates are distracted and begin to complain. Before long a reprimand has been received from the teacher. The ADD Syndrome child does not know why he or she is scolded all the time. "John, sit still!" he hears over and over. "Carl, stop making that noise!" he hears when he does not realize that he is making noise. Hyperactive ones are continually standing up at inappropriate moments, leaving the desk to walk across the room, going too often to the pencil sharpener, lingering at the library table instead of returning to the desk, staying too long in the restroom, and so forth. These restless children cannot stay put. The overflow body movement reflects the restless state of mind with which these children live. Their minds "fidget" the ways their bodies do. This physically restless overflow is a major earmark of ADD Syndrome.

## Poor Listening Comprehension

Ability to understand a stream of oral information is very poor with ADD Syndrome students. As a rule, the level of comprehension through listening is seldom higher than thirty percent. This means that the ADD Syndrome listener fully understands and retains only about one third of what he or she hears in the course of a school day. This deficit in auditory perception has nothing to do with the ability to hear. ADD Syndrome children usually hear well enough. The problem is that the central nervous system does not connect meaning to the flow of words that come through listening. Sometimes these children interrupt by making oral footnotes, which was described in Chapter One. Sometimes they respond with a puzzled "What?" or "Huh?" Sometimes they give no response at all as if they had heard nothing. When time lag is a factor, the student cannot develop a mental image rapidly enough to respond to what he or she just heard. Poor listening ability is a major obstacle in classroom performance for most ADD Syndrome students.

It is difficult for these children to participate in class discussions. The strands of oral information that are shared by several classmates during a discussion do not connect into a meaningful mental image for the ADD Syndrome listener. What John says does not connect with what Mary replies. The teacher's question has nothing to do with the answer recited by Paul. Again, the ADD Syndrome child is on an island within a stream of flowing talk. The sense of isolation increases as others converse or discuss because it makes no sense to the poor listener. This isolation in listening intensifies the emergence of boredom and restlessness. The ADD Syndrome child is lost in activities that require that oral language be processed and understood on another person's schedule.

Teachers face a continual problem in making new information clear to the ADD Syndrome listener. As the teacher explains a new procedure, gives oral instructions, or lectures on a specific topic, this child does not follow. Bits and pieces of the oral information may register, but the child does not develop a full mental image of what was said. This leaves him or her unable to put that oral information to use. As the teacher finishes giving instructions, she may ask: "Does everyone understand?" The ADD Syndrome child never does. The same hand goes up everytime, wanting to know what to do. The same voice is raised everytime: "What are we supposed to do?" If the teacher points out that the child is not following instructions, the ADD Syndrome child exclaims: "You never told me that," or "I didn't hear you say to do it." This scene is played again and again, hour after hour, day after day. The child's listening skills do not grow no matter how much scolding is done. The central nervous system of the ADD Syndrome listener is not capable of processing a flow of oral information and getting the full meaning of what was said to the group.

These poor listeners often do quite well in one-to-one relationships where the speaker watches for lost attention, then backs up and helps the child hear it again. One-to-one, the teacher can hold the child's thought patterns in tight enough focus to permit full understanding of what is heard. But in group activity where the child is left to do his or her own structuring, the attention span is too short. Without being tightly guided, the ADD Syndrome listener drifts and loses the continuity of what he or she is hearing.

### Unpredictable Response

One of the most frustrating characteristics of ADD Syndrome is the tendency to do some of the steps of the task well, then begin to make mistakes on the next steps in the same task. This is frequently seen in math computation.

Memory for math facts or how to carry or borrow is good for five or six problems at a time. Then the child misses the next several problems completely. On spelling tests, this student spells several words correctly, then suddenly misspells the next several words in a "careless" way. The time frame for doing fully accurate math or accurate spelling is short. This "short circuit" pattern is not caused by carelessness. As the student works through a series of tasks, specific memory becomes spotty and unpredictable. Clear mental images one moment become cluttered and confused the next moment. Students with these "short circuit" patterns seldom maintain fully clear thought images for more than several seconds at a time. These youngsters are at constant disadvantage doing assignments. No matter how hard they pledge to do better, their "short circuit" memory patterns trip them up. Promising to be more careful does not change this underlying neurological deficit.

This unpredictability in memory work is also seen in oral responses which the ADD Syndrome student is asked to give. Being required to give specific answers from memory is spotty and unpredictable. These students continually lose their words. For example, no matter how many times they may have named geometric shapes or math signs, they stumble when naming a triangle, a rectangle, a square, a plus sign, a minus sign, and so forth. When these "short circuits" occur, the student is forced to stop, wait, search for the lost word, then try to give the answer the teacher is waiting for. If time is limited, as in most intelligence tests and achievement tests, the student cannot earn credit when the memory search takes too long.

ADD Syndrome students suffer much embarrassment at home and at school when adults make an issue of their trouble giving answers. If the child is scolded for not answering well, he or she is once more humiliated by unpredictable ability to respond. These frequent cycles of being unable to answer accurately implant deep feelings of helplessness. This kind of invisible struggle with the names of things or with unexpected errors while working a string of problems does great damage to sensitive self-image. It is impossible for students with these memory deficits to develop positive self-image when they never know what will emerge when a specific response is called for.

## Poor Organization

Perhaps the most noticeable characteristic of ADD Syndrome is the inability to be organized. Chronically loose thought patterns make it impossible for the student to perceive how various parts should fit together. This student does not see how separate bits and pieces should be related into a well organized whole. Clothing lying around the room does not appear to this child as clutter. A sock on the chair is not seen as out of place, nor is the sweater lying on the floor. Each is an article of clothing that is worn or not worn, but the child does not perceive a sock on the floor as being out of place. Where the sock or shirt or pair of jeans is does not connect within the child's mind as being important. When mother commands the child to "go clean up your room," the ADD Syndrome child has no idea what mother means. The mental images of this child do not "see" individual things as being out of order because there is no overall perception of an organized whole.

This lack of mental organization is a major source of friction in the classroom. The tools of learning are not seen by the ADD Syndrome child as an organized, integrated whole. A book lying on the floor does not seem out of place. A pencil left on the library table is not connected with the writing task that was interrupted when the child went to sharpen the pencil. As the ADD Syndrome student moves through the day, there is no cumulative mental image of where things are or where they ought to be. In a homeroom class where the child stays all day, essential things are misplaced continually. When it is time for math, the math book is missing. When it is time for reading, yesterday's homework cannot be found. When it is time to draw, the crayons are not in the desk. Children in a departmentalized curriculum which requires the class to move to a different room each hour are at a serious disadvantage. If ADD Syndrome students must go to their lockers for new supplies several times a day, it is impossible for them to be on time to the next class. These students are forever tardy. If they must catch the bus immediately after school, they cannot remember what books to take home to do evening assignments. Parents who pick children up after school continually face the problem of something important being left behind. No amount of scolding or lecturing makes any difference. The central nervous system of the ADD Syndrome student cannot maintain an organized, long range image of duties and responsibilities unless a written list is made for each set of expectations. Even then, the ADD Syndrome child tends to lose the list. Poor organization is an earmark of this neurological deficit.

## Distractibility

When one is a member of a class group, progress depends upon being able to concentrate on the main activity while tuning out events that are not related to the central task. Children with normal neurological processing ability soon learn to ignore anything that is not important at that moment. ADD Syndrome youngsters cannot do so successfully. Little events, such as nearby sounds, unexpected activity across the room, some movement out of the corner of the eye, or a sudden new odor, clamor for the ADD Syndrome child's attention. The child darts off on that rabbit trail instead of saying "no" to the impulse. Eye control is lost at that moment, so the student loses the place in reading. Thought patterns are interrupted, so the student forgets what he or she was doing. Mental image of the task dissolves, leaving the student lost and wondering what to do after the distraction has been investigated.

It is impossible for these chronically distracted youngsters to finish the task. They continually leave jobs unfinished or assignments only partly done. They do not get all the way through a work page before attention is diverted. Then they do not manage to come back to finish the page. They tend to skip portions of the assignment, thinking that every step has been completed. Later when adults scan the unfinished work, conflict is triggered as the child is accused of being careless or not paying attention to the work. ADD Syndrome children leave holes in their work, not realizing that everything has not been done. Their impression recalls that the student was doing work. When he or she stopped working, it must have been because it was finished. These students do not have awareness that their attention was distracted. The small amount of work done seems to them to be the whole task.

### Burnout

Most ADD Syndrome students have specific, measurable points at which a type of burnout occurs. For example, it is not unusual to find a time cycle of three minutes, five minutes, or seven minutes during which full concentration on a task can be maintained. At the end of that time cycle, the student suddenly "loses everything." Often it is described as "going blank." This refers to the sudden loss of ability to think, to analyze, or to continue doing that task. Quality of work may have been quite good with few errors until burnout occurs, then suddenly everything is wrong and a radical change occurs in the quality of work. Good spelling falls apart. Smooth left-to-right sequencing begins to scramble. Accurate math computation becomes filled with errors. Memory for the procedure is gone, leaving the student fumbling and groping for what to do next. Sentence structure falls apart with fragments appearing instead of full sentence form. Typing errors suddenly multiply in the middle of smooth keyboard writing. Essay writing falls apart after getting off to a good start. Students with these burnout points are bewildered, not understanding what is happening. Teachers are puzzled, not understanding how this radical change can occur so frequently. Adults who watch these daily burnout patterns often realize that the student is doing his or her very best, yet the effort deteriorates after a certain length of time. Neurological "burnout" is one of the common problems of ADD Syndrome in the classroom.

## Emotional Sensitivity

Like students with other forms of specific learning disability, those with ADD Syndrome live on the edge of failure. No classroom task is free from the hovering threat of failure. Nothing they do is guaranteed not to fail. The quirks that continually block memory are like goblins dancing around the student's desk, threatening to cause mistakes at any moment. Students who live under this never ending shadow of defeat are understandably sensitive. From their earliest days in formal education, they have been publicly criticized for "not trying harder." Teachers have said many times: "You didn't follow my instructions. Don't you ever listen when I explain?" Parents have said more times than they can count: "I've told you a dozen times. Don't you ever hear what I say?" Adults and peers have made comments and jokes about how forgetful the student is. "John would lose his head if it weren't fastened on" stopped being funny years ago to the ADD Syndrome youngster. Being labeled "careless" or "lazy" is painful and embarrassing. Bearing that reputation as long as the child can remember is humiliating. Before the ADD Syndrome student has been in school very long, he or she has become quite emotional about these chronic accusations.

Hyperactive ADD Syndrome students usually become outwardly defensive. They storm out at those who criticize them. They start fights to avenge their honor. They scheme ways to get even with adversaries who tease or make sarcastic remarks. Many playground and lunchroom scuffles are triggered by an overly sensitive ADD Syndrome youngster fighting back. Tragically, many overly sensitive young people become involved in antisocial behavior that brings them under the jurisdiction of juvenile authority. Their destructive behavior began with classroom failure. After all, if a child does his or her best, but that best is never good enough, what is the child to do?

Passive ADD Syndrome students usually do not storm out in overt self-defense. They tend to pull back into themselves, tuning out the classroom atmosphere that inflicts so much pain through failure. They often become increasingly detached as their defense. If they do not hear what others say, they will not be hurt by what others say. In defending themselves so passively, they also cut themselves off from classroom participation. Formal learning stops, but at least overly sensitive feelings are spared. It is possible for ADD Syndrome students to build such thick, tough walls of passive self-protection that it becomes impossible for classroom teachers to reach through the barrier.

### Misunderstanding

The lives of most ADD Syndrome children are clouded by misunderstanding. They continually misunderstand what others say or mean. Others continually misunderstand their behavior. Well organized adults who have no difficulty with loose thought patterns cannot believe that the child, who is healthy and bright, cannot do better. Teachers and parents tend to interpret the ADD Syndrome behavior patterns as being disobedient, lazy, or not trying. Adults often try to force the disorganized child to function more effectively. However, no amount of discipline changes the patterns. If adults give too much supervision in order to get the child to function, others say that too much coddling is going on: "John has to

40

learn to accept responsibility on his own." If adults back away and place all responsibility upon the child, nothing improves. In fact, an ADD Syndrome child left alone to carry out responsibility is helpless.

Misunderstanding multiplies rapidly in the classroom. Instructions are misunderstood and not carried out by the ADD Syndrome child. Comments made by peers are misinterpreted and blown out of proportion by overly sensitive youngsters. Peers misunderstand the halting speech of the classmate who has lost his or her words in trying to tell about something. Diagnosticians and other professionals who try to evaluate the ADD Syndrome child often misunderstand, not seeing the overall syndrome. It would be accurate to say that most ADD Syndrome children are among the most seriously misunderstood youngsters within our culture. They live most of their developmental years being misunderstood and failing to understand the world around them.

### Insatiability

As described in Chapter One, the hyperactive ADD Syndrome child tends to be insatiable. Insatiable need for personal attention and approval becomes an enormous problem in the classroom. An insatiable student does not leave others alone. It is impossible for this child to study silently or alone. The need for feedback from others is overwhelming. The insatiable child clamors for the teacher's attention regardless of how much time the teacher has already spent one-to-one with him or her. This child cannot stay in a designated space without someone to share that space. The child cannot leave classmates alone during independent study time. The insatiable child must have continual contact through touching, speaking, and being spoken to. This student is overly sensitive about being alone. When teachers and classmates become frustrated and tell the insatiable one to leave them alone, his or her feelings are hurt. Sometimes there is an emotional outburst of self-defense as the rejected student blames others for being selfish or not caring. Sometimes he or she retreats into a pout, brooding about how unfair everyone always is. The insatiable child is extremely immature, unable to deal with the issues of life realistically.

The need for constant company overpowers every other need of the insatiable child. He or she runs extreme risks in order to have the attention of others. These children expose themselves to great risk of rejection or ridicule in order not to be isolated. An insatiable ADD Syndrome student is disruptive. This student places heavy pressure upon the emotions of the group. The insatiable child in the classroom demands much more than anyone can give. There is no concept of privacy or appreciation of the territorial rights of others. The inner hunger for response from others overwhelms all other considerations as these children clamor to be satisfied.

## Impact of Failure on Self-Esteem

Probably the most devastating result of ADD Syndrome is loss of self-esteem. As children progress through their developmental years, the normal pattern is to accumulate good stories to tell about personal success, prizes and awards received, praise that was earned, and so forth. ADD Syndrome children are mostly left out of this normal developmental process. They do not win prizes for good work. Their papers are not displayed proudly on the bulletin board. Their report cards are not laced with praise. In fact, most adult comments to an ADD Syndrome child are negative in some important ways: "John, you didn't follow my instructions again...Mary, you forgot to put your name on your paper again...Sam, this is the fourth time I have repeated my instructions. Don't you ever listen?...Shelly, you forgot to give me your homework again...Robert, your handwriting must be neater." This litany of criticism and complaint never ends for the ADD Syndrome child. From the earliest years he or she can remember, adults have been saying negative things about the child's behavior. There is no cumulative memory of praise and compliments and congratulations for jobs well done. ADD Syndrome students have few positive stories to tell. When they do tell stories, they often resort to make believe to compensate for their history of failure. Then they are frequently accused of "lying" or not telling the truth.

Having no good stories to tell leaves deep scars upon the youngster's self-esteem. If everyone else has good stories to tell, but the ADD Syndrome child does not, then the impression of self is negative and inferior. If everyone else succeeds in winning praise, but the ADD Syndrome child hears only criticism and blame, the impression of self is that "I am not good." In later years, those who outgrow the academic problems of ADD Syndrome and become good students as adults continue to labor under the burden of low self-esteem. Being unable to satisfy adult expectation during the important developmental years of childhood implants deeply rooted impressions that self is bad, inadequate, and of low value. The feeling of low self-worth is an unfortunate legacy when ADD Syndrome is not recognized early so that constructive help can be given.

### Messy Papers

Most ADD Syndrome students have trouble writing neatly and producing attractive written work. The central nervous system cannot maintain well organized thought patterns during the act of writing. Figure 1 illustrates this problem. This 13-year-old boy could not copy from the board accurately. He was not dyslexic, which also causes sloppy writing and mistakes in copying. Figure 1 shows the frequent "short circuits" that continually interrupted his mental image as he transferred visual information from the chalkboard to his paper. All of this boy's school work had this appearance. His spelling papers were filled with erasures and scratch-overs as he searched for a better way to write the word. Math papers were almost impossible to decipher because of so many errors in encoding. Book reports and other kinds of essay material were so sloppy his teachers wondered if he ever tried to be neat.

Boy: Age 13 years, 1 month

**Test 1**

**Daniel Boone was a courageous vigorous man. Years ago he entered the American wilderness with visions of all who would follow the trail he blazed. Westward migration did begin to move over his pathways through**

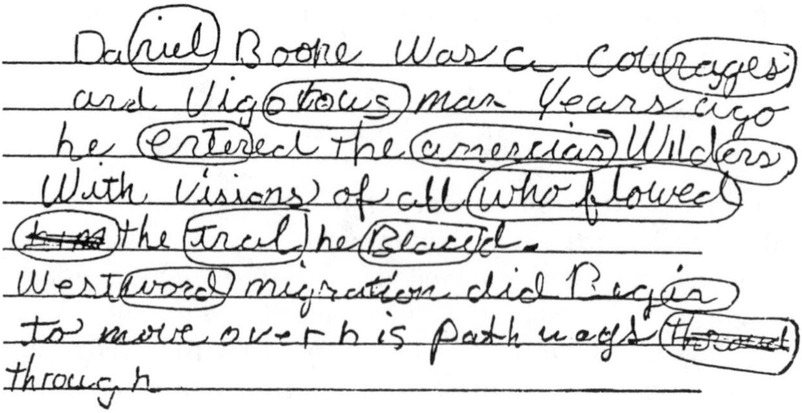

From Form D — Slingerland Screening Tests. Permission has been granted to reproduce this example.

**Figure 1.** Written work of 13-year-old boy.

The written work of ADD Syndrome students is continually criticized and condemned. If teachers have the practice of displaying the best papers on the bulletin board, these children almost never share the glory of public praise for good writing. Written work is usually so frustrating the child develops a system for losing or hiding classroom papers. Teachers often find desks or lockers stuffed with assignments never handed in. The child cannot take pride in his or her written work. It does not earn praise, and it often does not receive credit because of abundant errors and "careless" appearance. Fine motor coordination is often too unpredicatable to let these students do better. Copying papers over or doing written assignments again does not improve the quality. It is often impossible for these children to produce neat, well organized written work that is free from mistakes.

## Erratic Reading Comprehension

Most ADD Syndrome students have adequate phonetic skills. Unless they are also dyslexic, they do not have disability with phonics. They tend to stumble over syllables within words, and they cannot always keep sound units in the right sequence, but they usually know how to blend sounds together and how to chunk. Phonics skills are often among the highest skills we see in diagnostic testing of these students.

However, reading comprehension tends to be low and unpredictable. The problem is like that found in listening to oral information. In listening to a stream of speech, the central nervous system of the ADD Syndrome student does not process everything that is heard. Only bits and pieces of the oral flow are successfully changed into meaningful thought patterns and mental images. The same problem occurs as the child reads. He or she may be able to sound out or correctly recognize every word on the page, but only bits and pieces of the meaning are successfully recorded by the memory. The ADD Syndrome reader does not develop a cumulative, on-going mental image of what the text has said. The reader may be able to turn the printed passage into inner speech so that the author's writing becomes inner language for the child. However, the ADD Syndrome reader does not process this inner language of reading any better than he or she processes the oral flow of listening. The child leaves a reading task with only partial images of what was decoded. This makes it impossible for him or her to answer follow-up questions successfully.

The amount of material to be read is of critical importance for most ADD Syndrome students. Short attention and rapid burnout sabotage the task of reading large quantities of text material. If an analysis is done of the student's reading comprehension, wide fluctuations will be seen from page to page. A typical ADD Syndrome reading pattern might be 100% comprehension on the first page, 80% on the second page, and 40% on the third page. At that point the student must stop because the reading task has become too frustrating. If he or she comes back after a brief rest, the level of comprehension would usually be back to 80% or higher on the fourth page. Then it would start down again on the fifth page and reach burnout again on the sixth page. Careful analysis shows that the child had excellent reading comprehension part of the time but very poor reading comprehension at other times within the same block of reading. Overall reading ability continually zig-zags from high to low as time passes during the act of silent reading. It is impossible for these loose thinkers to benefit from sustained reading tasks. However, they can do quite good reading if the text is divided into segments that fit the cycles of neurological burnout. This kind of planning can be plotted for ADD Syndrome children if diagnostic attention is given to the cycles which differ from student to student.

# Avoidance of Work

One of the most difficult problems teachers face in dealing with ADD Syndrome students is keeping them at their work. Because of boredom, short attention, drifting away from the task, and so forth, these children face school work with great dread. If they are overly sensitive about possibly being wrong, they often develop emotional phobias when there is the chance they might make mistakes. Many ADD Syndrome students develop deep seated habits of avoiding their work. They cannot tolerate the normal pressure of academic toil. They are too easily overwhelmed by the emotional surges involved with frequent failures. They spend a great deal of time and energy seeking ways to get out of doing the assignment. Some ADD Syndrome children continually complain of "not feeling well." This can be based in very real discomfort from eye strain. If poor vision is an actual problem, then the child does indeed have frequent headaches and not feel well. If the child fits the Shoestring Baby category, which was described in Chapter One, immaturity of the digestive system or intestinal allergy to certain foods may cause gastric problems that keep the child's digestive tract in misery. However, most avoiders do not have actual physical problems. The plea to "go to the restroom" or "go see the nurse" is usually an effort to avoid tasks that place too much stress on fragile skills.

These children avoid tasks any way they can. Pencil leads are broken every few minutes, requiring frequent trips to the pencil sharpener. It is easy to stretch a 45 second pencil sharpening chore into two or three minutes away from the desk. Or the child may want to look up a word in the unabridged dictionary that is across the room in the library area. This simple chore can be extended into a quarter hour search. Or the student may have left an essential item in the locker and ask for a hall pass. Once out of the room, it is easy to stretch a locker visit into half an hour. The fact that the student invariably ends up in trouble for this kind of pro-crastination makes no difference in the avoidance patterns. Avoiding threatening work is worth the consequence.

Passive ADD Syndrome students often develop another type of avoidance. Instead of overtly leaving the scene of the task, they silently drift away into "daydreams." Sometimes they develop cover-up behavior of seeming to do the work while actually nothing is accomplished. They learn how to "look busy" from across the room while spending the time adrift in a world of wishful make believe. Later they must face the consequences of work not finished, but their passive drifting helps pass the time without becoming involved in doing the task. It is possible for these silent drifters to float for a year or longer before adults become aware that no skill development is taking place. If the student does just enough to avoid failing the class, he or she might float for several years, learning nothing new nor increasing important skills. The avoidance behavior of ADD Syndrome students is some-times beyond the reach of the classroom teacher. If the tendency becomes too deep seated, there may be nothing effective the teacher can do to change the student's response to school work.

These are the faces of ADD syndrome in the classroom. The surface behavior appears lazy, disinterested, unmoti-vated, and careless. The child may drive everyone crazy by clamoring constantly, or he or she may simply drift in a silent way, intellectually apart from the mainstream learning taking place in the classroom. Scolding does not change the behavior. Forcing the child to work without help does no good. Poor organization, messy papers, and lost materials continue to frustrate both the teacher and student day after day. Punishment does not bring better performance. Unless the underlying neurologically based problem is identified, years of conflict and a life of chronic failure are set into motion with devastating effects upon self-esteem.

---
---

---

## CHAPTER THREE:

## How to Help Attention Deficit Disorder

Those who rear, guide, or teach children with Attention Deficit problems must remember the severity scale presented in Chapter One:

| 0 | 1 2 3 | 4 5 6 7 | 8 9 10 |
|:---:|:---:|:---:|:---:|
| none | mild | moderate | severe |

Youngsters who display ADD Syndrome patterns at the severe level usually need medication along with strict diet control before they can become teachable. Those who are within the moderate range can be taught and influenced if certain kinds of structure are maintained in their lives. Persons with mild Attention Deficit patterns can get by successfully by being reminded when they are forgetful. The following guidelines can make the difference between success or failure as adults attempt to handle these patterns in children and adolescents.

### 1. MEDICATION

Sometimes it is necessary to medicate children with severe Attention Deficit Disorder. Most professionals are reluctant to take this step for fear that prolonged medication might inhibit normal growth and development of the child. However, youngsters at the severe level of Attention Deficit cannot interact successfully with their world, nor can they control themselves. When it is clear that a hyperactive child is beyond control or that a child's mental processes are too loose to let him or her be a successful part of family, school, or community, medication may be the only solution for that time in the child's life. A rule of thumb can help parents decide when to seek medical help for Attention Deficit Disorder: IF A HYPERACTIVE OR PASSIVE CHILD IS CLEARLY BEYOND THE REACH OF ADULT LEADERSHIP, AND IF THAT CHILD CLEARLY CANNOT SUCCEED SOCIALLY, EDUCATIONALLY, AND EMOTIONALLY THE WAY THINGS ARE, THEN IT IS TIME TO CONSULT A MEDICAL SPECIALIST FOR HELP. Many pediatricians now specialize in the control of Attention Deficit Disorder, although most physicians pay attention only to the hyperactive form of this problem (4, 18, 19). Several medications are available to help reduce hyperactivity, increase attention span, and decrease distractibility. Ritalin is preferred by many specialists. Cylert is also frequently used. Depending upon a child's body chemistry, neither of these medications may be successful. We often have to do trial-and-error medication before the right one is found. The point of medication is not to sedate the child or subdue the personality. The purpose of medication for Attention Deficit Disorder is to lengthen attention span, decrease conflict with the environment, and open up the child's intelligence for more effective learning. If medication is the only way to accomplish these goals, then it is well worth doing. When children are at the severe level of ADD Syndrome, they are helpless to improve their behavior. Parents run grave risk of life-long personality disorders if a child goes year after year under the heavy burden of constant failure, being a misfit, and forever being scolded for behaviors he or she cannot control.

2. DIET CONTROL

A great deal of controversy arises whenever diet control is suggested to reduce hyperactivity and distractibility. Yet those of us who work with large numbers of struggling learners see many students who have cytotoxic reactions to certain foods, beverages, and food additives. A growing number of pediatricians and

50

psychiatrists are aware that within the student population, a sizable number of struggling learners do react negatively to such food substances as refined white sugar, refined white wheat products, milk, certain fruits (especially grapes and grape products), caffeine in dark soda beverages, chemical additives, and dyes. Clinicians, parents, and teachers often see dramatic changes in student behavior when cytotoxic elements are taken out of the child's diet. In spite of the lack of absolute "proof" from research studies, those of us on the firing line trying to deal with Attention Deficit Disorder see the devastating consequences certain students experience when they take culprit foods or chemicals into their bodies. When a child is at the severe level of ADD Syndrome, parents should give serious consideration to controlling the diet of the youngster. Parents should search their communities for a pediatrician who recognizes this problem and is prepared to work with families in diet control techniques.

## 3. TIGHT STRUCTURE

The basic problem of Attention Deficit Disorder is that the person has no internal structure to guide him or her dependably. Thought patterns are too loose to stay on a constructive course very long. Memory is too spotty and unreliable to let rules and regulations guide the person's behavior from day to day. It is impossible for an ADD Syndrome person to live a consistently regular, orderly life without outside help.

The greatest need any ADD Syndrome person faces is for someone else to help keep things organized and on schedule. Parents must become the source of the child's organization. Teachers must provide consistent guidelines that tell the child what to do. Any adult in a leadership position must be the eyes and ears of the ADD Syndrome person, especially one who is at Level 5 or higher on the severity scale. This requires extraordinary patience on the part of the adult. New mercies must be extended over and over without punishing the child for memory failure or poor organization. Adults must remember that this child cannot help being forgetful, disorganized, overly active, overly passive, or too loose to plug into his or her world successfully. Certain basic strategies must be maintained by adults if these loose thinkers are to get safely through their struggling years before they begin to outgrow the syndrome.

### Written Lists of Responsibilities

ADD Syndrome youngsters cannot remember what they are told. That is a major earmark of the problem. Chapter One described the incredibly poor listening comprehension we find in most ADD Syndrome children and adults. They seldom retain more than one third of what they hear unless it is repeated and reinforced. The most effective way to guide a child with Attention Deficit Disorder is to follow up all oral instructions with written lists and outlines. If the child is expected to do three things, then the adult must make a list of those specific tasks. Each task should be numbered so the child has a brief visible outline:

1. Make your bed.
2. Empty the trash.
3. Feed the dog.

This kind of task outline should be posted some place where the child will be several times during the day: on the refrigerator, on the bedroom door, on the family bulletin board, on the bathroom mirror. Then the adult consistently reminds the child: "Have you done everything on your list?" This brief verbal reminder sends the child back to the list to check his or her progress. At school, teachers make lists of assignments, projects that will be due on certain dates, materials the child needs to take home, and so forth. These brief lists are taped to the child's desktop or wherever the student will spend most of the day. Again, the teacher continually reminds the child: "John, have you done everything on your list? Do you have all of your books gathered up to take home?" This kind of monitoring of an ADD Syndrome child is usually required until middle teens. About Age 14 most Attention Deficit youngsters begin to remember better on their own. Some continue to need this kind of help into their late teens or early twenties. The point is that they cannot stay organized without help because their internal patterns are too loose.

## Supervision

It is impossible for moderately or severely ADD Syndrome children to function without being supervised. Adults simply cannot walk away and leave these younsters to carry out tasks on their own. It has been explained in Chapters One and Two that memory patterns, sense of cause and effect, and awareness of how parts go together to make a whole are faulty in these youngsters. They cannot perceive when their rooms are a mess. They cannot see when the school desk or locker should be cleaned out. They do not notice when their stuff is scattered all over the house. They cannot maintain orderly space unless they are supervised. It is impossible for an ADD Syndrome youngster to "go clean up your room." Nor can an Attention Deficit child "go straighten up the garage." Memory patterns are simply too loose and disorganized for this kind of self-directed work. Adults face the task of working with an ADD Syndrome child, not just giving orders. If John's room is cluttered, mom or dad must actually be with him and show him how to put things away. If Susie's room or desk or personal space is a mess, she must have help getting it straight. The adult must stay right there, giving one instruction at a time: "Now, John, let's find all your socks. No, John, leave those books alone for right now. We are looking just for socks. Don't bother about your jeans just yet. Let's keep on looking just for socks." This very specific direction guides the child in finding all of the socks. Then the adult guides him in organizing another specific item. The room is finally put in order step-by-step as the adult helps the child focus his or her attention on one specific object at a time. Otherwise, the child is distracted by everything at once. Adults must remember what Attention Deficit is. It is the inability to keep mental images clearly focused longer than a few seconds at a time. It is the inability to ignore whatever is on the edge. This kind of supervision must be provided anytime an ADD Syndrome child is expected to carry out responsibility. This includes doing dishes, taking a bath, shampooing hair, mowing the yard, picking up dad's tools, getting home with all the necessary books for homework, returning homework to school next day, and so forth. Anytime an adult expects an ADD syndrome child to follow through from start to finish, the child must be supervised. It is impossible for him or her to achieve success any other way.

## Allowance for Immaturity

One of the most obvious problems of ADD Syndrome children is their immaturity. Most youngsters with Attention Deficit Disorder are bright. In fact, a majority of these strugglers demonstrate average to superior intelligence on IQ tests if the adult giving the test knows how to work with these attentional deficits. Most ADD Syndrome children have one or two academic areas in which they excel when they have enough supervision to finish assignments. Many of them are highly creative. Yet they behave like much younger children. For example, John is a Level 7 ADD Syndrome child. He is nine years old. He is bright with IQ 117 (Mental Age 11 years, 9 months). He is good at spelling (5th grade, 4th month level), and he is in the third month of 4th grade (Grade 4.3). Reading Comprehension is excellent when he is settled down enough to concentrate (7th grade, 3rd month level). Math skills are average at early 4th grade level. But he acts like a six-year-old much of the time when it comes to fitting into his class, taking his turn, sharing with others, and accepting responsibility. He fidgets, squirms, irritates his classmates, complains about having too much work to do, interrupts, and cannot stay on task without constant reminding. John's maturity profile would look like this:

| | | |
|---|---|---|
| Reading Age | 12 | beginning 7th grade |
| Mental Age | 11½ | middle 6th grade |
| Spelling Age | 10½ | middle 5th grade |
| Chronological Age | 9½ | middle 4th grade |
| Math Age | 9 | beginning 4th grade |
| Attention Span Age | 7 | beginning 2nd grade |
| Emotional Maturity Age | 6½ | middle 1st grade |

Most adults try to work with Attention Deficit children backwards. Adults traditionally see how old the child is, where he or she is in school, how well the child can read, and how high the intelligence is. Adults tend to expect that child to behave and achieve on those higher levels. This approach does not work with ADD Syndrome youngsters. The only way to have a successful relationship with such a child is to deal with him or her the opposite way. If this bright, alert child has the attention span of a little one in 2nd grade, and if this nine-year-old boy has the emotional maturity of a 1st grade pupil, then the adult must begin at that point. In other words, children like John must be guided, nurtured, sheltered, structured, and disciplined the way adults expect to deal with a bright six-year-old boy.

Attention Deficit youngsters always show this kind of spread between their highest levels of abilities and their lowest levels of maturity. If they are to find success, they must not be judged by their highest areas. They must be guided as if they were much younger. John's parents must structure his life the way they would if he were actually six years old. They must keep him out of situations that demand the emotional maturity of older children. They must not let him become involved in activities in which he will surely fail or will become overly frustrated or be regarded as a nuisance by leaders and peers. To place such a bright, sensitive, but immature boy in activities designed for nine-year-

55

olds is to guarantee that he will be humiliated and over-stressed. Adults are asking for trouble when they ignore the maturity level of the ADD Syndrome child.

The critical factor for John is the extreme difference between his ability to read and think and his ability to control his emotions and maintain good attention. It is usually devastating for children with this much developmental difference to be enrolled in team sports for their age group. They cannot follow coaches' instructions, they cannot remember what to do on the playing field, they cannot handle the emotional pressures of winning and losing, and they cannot be good partners in sharing and taking turns. Parents of ADD Syndrome children must allow for immaturity. Most youngsters with Attention Deficit Disorder begin to catch up in emotional maturity as puberty brings the body forward in physical development. But few ADD Syndrome youngsters are as mature as their age until their middle or late teens. When they do not outgrow these patterns (Attention Deficit Disorder, Residual Type), they become adults still performing emotionally on the level of a child.

### Help With School Work

A major principle in working with ADD Syndrome learners is this: A STUDENT WITH ATTENTION DEFICIT DISORDER MUST HAVE HELP WITH ASSIGNMENTS. These students are too loose, too poorly organized, and too distractible to study silently by themselves. Again, parents and teachers must keep the immaturity factor in mind. How well can a six-year-old child study alone? How much school work can a seven-year-old do without help and supervision? Until physical development is complete in the late teens or early twenties, ADD Syndrome students must have help to study, learn new information, prepare for tests, and finish projects. They simply cannot function academically all alone. It is counterproductive for parents to send a child with Attention Deficit to his or her room with orders to "study for an hour."

Few ADD Syndrome students manage ten good minutes of productive study out of an hour if they are alone. Most of them need a study partner at school, someone to sit nearby to answer questions, interpret instructions, and help them come back to the main track when they drift off on rabbit trails. Parents must be within touching distance as these youngsters do homework for the same reason. The only way an ADD Syndrome student at Level 5 or higher can study is to have a companion. Even if no words are exchanged, the physical presence of someone nearby helps immensely in keeping the student's attention focused on the task. If this child is alone, almost nothing is accomplished except star gazing, rabbit trailing, and time lost off in his or her world of make-believe.

### Consistent Discipline

Attention Deficit children must have discipline. This does not mean spankings or rough scoldings. Discipline for these youngsters means that adults maintain consistent rules and limits. A list is made of whatever the limits need to be:

1. Do not go into your sister's room without permission
2. Do not play with mom's or dad's things without permission.
3. Do not ride your bike down the street without permission.

Whatever parents feel are necessary rules, these must be carefully explained and discussed until the child understands what the limits are. Then certain consequences must be invoked whenever the rules are broken. If John continues to mess with his sister's things without her permission, certain discipline will follow. If he rides his bike to forbidden areas, then certain consequences will take place. It is absolutely essential that adults maintain discipline for these youngsters who have such poor sense of organization and order. Each family must establish its own form of discipline. Ideally, a child should never be disciplined when the parent is angry. But adults cannot always do what is ideal. The goal should be that the adults be ready to invoke whatever consequences were announced ahead of time. Sometimes ADD Syndrome children respond best to being isolated from the rest of the family until they can calm down or think things through. Sometimes they should be grounded from doing favorite things when they break the rules. Sometimes they respond to having to do extra chores. But whatever the rules are, the child must be disciplined when he or she deliberately steps over the line. Adults must be very careful to make sure that the forgetful, loose, poorly organized child actually disobeyed rather than simply forgot. ADD Syndrome children continually trespass into forbidden territory because they are too immature to read the "Keep Out" signs. But they must have enough consistent discipline to keep them out of danger and to help them learn that there are limits to be observed.

### Professional Help

Parents of Attention Deficit children often must have help. A child with severe Attention Deficit Disorder (Level 8 or 9) places enormous stress upon the marriage and all the relationships within the home and family. At times the task of coping with ADD syndrome is more than parents can handle alone. It is very important for parents to investigate potential professional help before becoming involved with a counselor or specialist. The least effective procedure is to judge the professional person by his or her credentials. It tells nothing at all about that person's effectiveness in dealing with ADD Syndrome to know what degrees he or she has from what school. The most effective way for parents to find good professional help is to ask other parents. Attention Deficit Disorder is a common problem. In any community, there will be other families struggling with the syndrome. The most obvious ADD children are the hyperactive ones who attract immediate attention wherever they are. The most difficult to help are the passive ones who drift away into their private worlds of silent make-believe. But it does not take long to discover several parents who have found effective help from specific agencies. Public reputation is often the most reliable way for parents to locate help. When several parents have been helped to manage this problem successfully, word spreads quickly. Parents do need to seek fully qualified professionals, of course, but the primary concern should be how effective that professional is with Attention Deficit Disorder children. Traditional psychotherapy has very little effect in changing Attention Deficit. Adults must remember that this is a brain-based disorder, not just a matter of laziness or stubbornness. The most effective professionals (counselors, pediatricians, mental health therapists) are those who view Attention Deficit Disorder from the point of view that the central nervous system is behind schedule reaching expected maturity. The approach to helping the ADD Syndrome child is to teach parents how to guide and discipline more effectively. Parents need to search for professional help that teaches them how to nurture children like John whose intelligence is so far ahead of his emotions.

# REFERENCES

1. Adams, Milton. *"Management of Attention Deficit Disorder,"* JOURNAL OF THE NATIONAL MEDICAL ASSOCIATION, Vol. 75, No. 2, 1983.
2. American Psychiatric Association. DIAGNOSTIC AND STATISTICAL MANUAL OF MENTAL DISORDERS, Third Edition, 1980.
3. Bland, Jeffrey. *"The Junk Food Syndrome,"* PSYCHOLOGY TODAY, Jan. 1982.
4. Bloomingdale, Lewis M. ATTENTION DEFICIT DISORDER. Spectrum Publications: Jamaica, New York, 1984.
5. Brown, Catherine Caldwell, ed. CHILDHOOD LEARNING DISABILITIES AND PRENATAL RISK. Pediatric Round Table 9: Johnson and Johnson Baby Products Company, 1983.
6. Clements, Samuel D. MINIMAL BRAIN DYSFUNCTION IN CHILDREN. Washington, D.C. U.S. Dept. H.E.W., Public Health Service Bulletin No. 1415 NINDS Monograph No. 3, 1966.
7. Gross, Mortimer B. and Wilson, William C. MINIMAL BRAIN DYSFUNCTION. Brunner/Mazel Publishers: New York, 1974.
8. Hagerman, Randi J. DEVELOPMENTAL PEDIATRICS. New Frontiers Symposium, Steamboat Springs, Colorado, 1983.
9. Jordan, Dale R. JORDAN PRESCRIPTIVE/TUTORIAL READING PROGRAM. PRO-ED, 8700 Shoal Creek Blvd., Austin, Texas 78758, 1988.
10. Jordan et al. Unpublished research at Jordan Diagnostic Center, Oklahoma City, Oklahoma, 1973-1987.
11. Menninger Foundation Symposium. LEARNING DISABILITIES: The Interface Between Brain-Based Dysfunctions and Adult Psychiatric Disturbances, Topeka, Kansas, 1985.

12. MENTAL HEALTH LETTER, *"Attention Deficit Disorder,"* The Harvard Medical School, Vol. 2, No. 3, Sept. 1985.

13. Nichamin, Samuel J. and Windell, James. A NEW LOOK AT ATTENTION DEFICIT DISORDER. Minerva Press: Waterford, Maine, 1984.

14. Ochroch, Ruth. THE DIAGNOSIS AND TREATMENT OF MINIMAL BRAIN DYSFUNCTION IN CHILDREN. Human Sciences Press: New York, 1981.

15. Powers, Hugh W. S. Jr. *"Dietary Measures to Improve Behavior and Achievement,"* ACADEMIC THERAPY, Vol. IX, No. 3.

16. SUPERVISING ADULTS WITH LEARNING DISABILITIES. President's Committee on Employment of the Handicapped: Washington, D.C., 1985.

17. von Hilshimer, George. ALLERGY, TOXINS, AND THE LEARNING DISABLED CHILD. Acadmic Therapy Publications: San Rafael, California, 1974.

18. Wild, C. Thomas. HOW TO CURE HYPERACTIVITY: Attention Span Advancement Registry Service: 1940 Fifth Avenue, Sacramento, California 95818, 1981.

19. Wild. C. Thomas. WHAT'S THE BEST WAY TO DEAL WITH HYPERACTIVITY? A New Update on The Attention Deficit Disorder (ADD). ASA, 1940 Fifth Avenue, Sacramento, California 95818, 1984.

20. Wunderlich, Ray C. Jr. ALLERGY, BRAINS, AND CHILDREN COPING. St. Petersburg, Florida: Johnny Reads, Inc. 1973.